THE JESSE TREE R

This month of readings is named afte
stained glass or wood that have bee
centuries to bring to life the characte~~rs who are part o~~.
Jesus' family tree from Jesse through David to Joseph and
Mary.

In many homes and churches it has become an Advent
custom to use a small tree branch as a Jesse Tree which is
either stripped and painted gold, white or silver, or left in
its natural state, and then hung with pictures or ornaments
representing the people, prophecies and stories which
anticipated the coming of Christ.

Some churches have a special Jesse Tree service, during
which the whole series of stories is recalled, and the
ornaments added, one by one. At home it is probably more
beneficial to take one reading, with its accompanying
Scriptures, per day, adding the ornaments as you go
through the month so that, rather like the pictures in an
Advent calendar, more and more appear as Christmas
approaches.

Some of the drawings and readings remind us of Jesus
through Noah, Jacob, Judah, Rahab, Ruth, Jesse, David,
Solomon and Zerubbabel. Some instead are rich in
prophetic significance, and recall the blood of Abel, the
forgiving love of Joseph, the resurrection of Jonah and
Isaiah's foretelling of the reign of the Prince of Peace.
The remaining days of December continue the story,
and also mark the feasts of Stephen, the 'holy innocents'
slaughtered by Herod, and John the beloved. They remind
us of the covenant that Jesus, the promised Messiah, invites
us all to enter into with Him.

The Jesse Tree can become a much loved focal point during December that can offset and pre-empt the onset of an increasingly commercial and secularised Christmas. We hope these readings and ornaments will help you to share in this age-old practice and provide a focus for prayer and memory, a spur to the imagination, and that the journey through image and Scripture in this month of December will again enkindle a flame of love and wonder as we enjoy the coming of Jesus, the promised One.

Andy Raine

DECEMBER 1

Psalm 72:17 Genesis 1:2–4, Matthew 5:44–45

THE SUN

The people of the islands of the Hebrides called the sun
'the eye of the great God'
because God looks on us
in warmth and love,
giving us life and light.
And they would bow the head
in reverence to God.

I bow my head to You, Lord God
who made the sun, and all that lives.
You are the true light –
a light which touches
every person born into the world.

DECEMBER 2

Psalm 8:3–9 Genesis 2:15–17; 3:1–13 Revelation 22:1–2

THE FRUIT OF THE TREE

'Are you sure that God said, No?
Aren't you grown-up enough to
make your own decisions?
One little taste won't hurt;
besides, you might like it.'

Then suddenly we know
only too well,
and begin to make excuses –
'It's not my fault...'
'I didn't mean it...'
'I couldn't help it...'
'The temptation was too great...'

DECEMBER 3

Psalm 22:9–11 Genesis 4:1–11 Colossians 1:19–20

ABEL

'Am I my brother's keeper?' asked Cain.
He should have cared for his younger brother
and looked out for him.
But he didn't.
Instead, he was jealous and killed him.
And the blood of Abel cried out to God
from the ground where he fell.

Jesus watches out for us like an elder brother.
He was killed by jealous men,
and His blood which fell from the cross to the ground
still cries out to the Father,
'Forgive them! They don't know what they are doing.'

And what about me?
Am I my brother's keeper?

DECEMBER 4

Psalm 105:7 Genesis 6:13–14 Hebrews 11:7

NOAH'S ARK

The people thought that Noah was a fool.
He built a wooden boat called an ark,
miles away from the sea.
Noah warned the people that God was angry
with all the evil things they did.
God was sad that they didn't want to love Him
and trust Him
like Noah and his family did.

Then the rain came, just as Noah had said.
Noah could shelter in the ark
just as God had shown him.
When the water covered the land
and reached the ark,
the ark floated on top of the waters.

DECEMBER 5

Psalm 105:8 Genesis 22:2, 6–14 Romans 8:31–32

THE SON ON THE ALTAR

'Abraham, your son must be killed –
your son, your only son,
the son you love.'
'Oh, God,' said Abraham,
'You don't know what it means
to give your son like that.'
But Abraham gave his son,
the son he loved;
and Isaac's life was spared.

God loved the world so much
that He gave His only Son;
so whoever believes and trusts
in Him will no longer be dying,
but come alive in Jesus.

DECEMBER 6

Psalm 105:9 Genesis 24:10–20, 55–59, 62–66 John 4:7, 13–15

THE CAMEL AND THE WATER JAR

Rebekah leaves her home and family
and trusts in God
who is bringing her to a man
she has never met,
but is to love and marry.
'I will go,' she says,
'let nothing hold me back
from the new life
that is waiting for me.'

She journeys into the desert
with a heart that reaches forward
and waits to give itself to love.

DECEMBER 7

Psalm 105:10–11 Genesis 28:10–17 Luke 2:13–14

THE LADDER

Heaven is not far away
if only our eyes were open
to see how kind God's heart is.
His messengers bring peace,
and tell us that God
wants all that is best for us.
Heaven is not far away,
and surely the Lord is here
where we are.

DECEMBER 8

Psalm 105:5–6 Genesis 49:1–2, 9–10 Revelation 5:1–14

THE LION BANNER

The King is coming!
He is called the Lion,
the Lion of the tribe of Judah;
and all the people
will gather to Him.
He came to us, gave us His life;
He lives again;
and He will come in glory!

DECEMBER 9

Psalm 105:12–22 Genesis 37:3–13 Luke 1:76–77

THE COAT OF MANY COLOURS

Joseph's coat is brightest of all.
Joseph is the chosen one,
honoured more than his brothers.
Joseph is the prophet, the dreamer of dreams;
chosen for honour, chosen for disgrace,
chosen to suffer.
Joseph was true to God and
true to his dreams.
It meant nakedness, shame,
reproach and false accusation.

Do I dare
be a dreamer for God's kingdom?

DECEMBER 10

Psalm 105:26–27 Exodus 3:2–5 Luke 1:34–35

THE BURNING BUSH

When Moses was tending his father-in-law's flocks,
out on the edge of the desert,
suddenly the angel of the Lord appeared to him
as a flame of fire in a bush.
When Moses saw the bush was on fire
and that it didn't burn up,
he went over to investigate.
Then God spoke to him out of the flame:
'Moses! Moses!'
'Who is it?' Moses asked.
'Don't come any closer,' God told him.
'Take off your shoes,
for you are standing on holy ground,
and I am God who speaks to you.'

God, when I know You're really here,
then where I stand is holy ground!

DECEMBER 11

Psalm 105:37–39 Exodus 13:17–22 1 Corinthians 10:1–3

THE PILLAR OF CLOUD AND FIRE

The presence of the Lord
went out before His people
to guide them.
By day, it would be as
a pillar of cloud;
by night the cloud was on fire.
When the cloud moved
they continued their journey;
when it stopped
they did not dare go further,
but waited for the cloud.

DECEMBER 12

Psalm 105:40b Exodus 16:14–15, 31–33 1 Corinthians 10:1–3

MANNA

God had called them to follow Him:
He led them into the desert.
He knew what they needed.
He provided for them.
They said, 'What is this?'
but they didn't go hungry,
and when they tasted
the bread He provided
its taste was sweet.

DECEMBER 13

THE TABLETS OF THE LAW

These Laws begin to show us
what God is like,
and how we can begin to be like Him.
Jesus showed us even more clearly:
we should love the Lord our God
with all our heart and strength,
and we should want the best
for everyone we know –
and even for those we have not met.

This is the beginning
of the fulfilling
of the Law which tells us
how to love.

DECEMBER 14

Psalm 36:7 Exodus 25:17–22; 35:30–35 Hebrews 9:3–5; 10:19–20

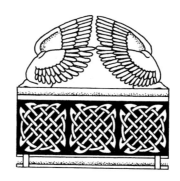

THE ARK OF THE COVENANT

God speaks to us in pictures:
smoke and glory; angels' wings;
light eternal; holy, radiant light
in the centre of all things,
the hidden place behind the veil.

Can God be held, contained
in a box of gold and wood?
Look! God makes His home
here among the people:
the hidden focus of our life.

DECEMBER 15

Psalm 98:2 Joshua 2:1–21; 6:20–25 Hebrews 11:31

THE SCARLET CORD

Rahab was told by the spies
to hang a scarlet thread
in the window of her house.
Just as the death-angel passed over
the houses of the Israelites
when blood was on the door,
so she would be saved
when the walls came down.
These two men had understood
the importance of the blood.

The scarlet thread stretches
through all of Scripture
and through all time,
saying: Sin means death,
but life is in the blood.

The blood of Jesus touches me;
I live, and I am free.

DECEMBER 16

Psalm 98:3 Ruth 2:2–9, 14–19; 3:7–9; 4:13–17 Matthew 9:36–38

THE EAR OF WHEAT

The ear of wheat speaks to us about harvest:
what we sow, and what we reap.
We remember the faithfulness of Ruth
who followed Naomi to her home, and cared for her.
God saw her faithfulness, and rewarded her.
He took her from the edges of the field
and placed her in the master's house –
made her the joy of his heart.

DECEMBER 17

Psalm 98:4 Micah 5:2, 4 Luke 2:15–18

BETHLEHEM

O Bethlehem,
you are but a small village in Judah;
yet you will be the birthplace of my King
who is alive from everlasting ages past!
And He shall stand and feed His flock
in the strength of the Lord,
in the majesty of the name of the Lord our God;
and His people shall remain there undisturbed,
for He will be greatly honoured
all around the world.

He will be our peace.

DECEMBER 18

Psalm 78: 70–72; 98:5 1 Samuel 16:1–12 Luke 2:8–11, 16, 20

SHEEP

Because the Lord is my shepherd
I have everything that I need.
He lets me rest in fresh meadows,
and leads me along beside quiet streams.
He helps me get better,
and I listen for His call.

DECEMBER 19

Psalm 98:6 2 Chronicles 6:12–15, 18–21 Acts 7:44–50

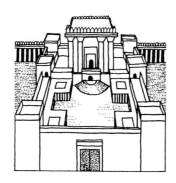

THE TEMPLE

Solomon made a home for God –
the most beautiful, the most splendid –
where He could be honoured
and praised
and remembered
and worshipped!
But earth itself or even heaven
could never hold the Almighty
who made them all:
the heavens, the earth,
the temple of Solomon,
could only hold a little
of the glory.

But God Himself
in all His splendour
can squeeze Himself
into a human heart
that is His throne.

DECEMBER 20

Psalm 98:7 Jonah 1:1–4; 2:10–3:10 Matthew 4:16

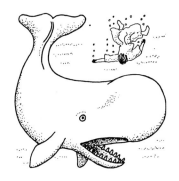

THE WHALE

Where could I run
to get away from You, God?
You've known this game
of hide and seek
for so very long.
At last I give up.
You win.
What was it, this secret
that You wanted me to tell?
The promise:
that You never give up.
You keep on seeking
those who hide from Your love.

DECEMBER 21

Psalm 72:5–7 Isaiah 52:7 Luke 1:26–33, 78–79

PEACE

The prophets said someone was coming
to be the hero all the people needed
to save them, and to champion the weak,
to teach the world about justice
and to bring us all peace.
Isaiah said:
To us a child is born:
we have a son.
He will carry His own throne
on His shoulders.
What are we to call Him?
Wonderful! Counsellor! Mighty God!
The Forever Father!
And for always the Prince of Peace!

DECEMBER 22

Psalm 98:8–9 Zechariah 4:6–10 Matthew 1:12–16; 5:14–16

ZERUBBABEL

Many obstacles stood in his way,
but the time was getting closer.
A longing grew in the hearts of many
to be again a people touched by God.
Zerubbabel was called to be a builder,
but not alone; for many hands must build
a temple for the Lord,
and many hearts determine
to begin the journey,
seek out the ancient paths,
move every mountain in the way.
Only the Spirit of God can bring
the miracle, and let them raise this house:
a beacon of glory on a hill.

DECEMBER 23

Psalm 72:8–11 Job 9:9–10 Matthew 2:1–2, 7–10

THE STAR

All peoples, all nations shall honour Him.
His love is so great it aches to receive
the homage of every heart.

A star led the travellers to Jesus.
They were seeking for the one life
that could make a difference
in their own lives –
that kind of journey always
changes you for ever.

Jesus, now I've found You,
let me be like that bright star
showing the way to others
who wonder where You are.

DECEMBER 24

Psalm 72:15 Isaiah 53:10–12 Luke 2:19, 34–35

CROWN AND SCEPTRE

- CROSS AND CROWN

This night, the long night,
the Christ-child will be born –
born to be King, born to die.
Joy comes through the pain –
there is no other way.
Through the long night
we wait in hope.
Cross and crown
bring shadow and light
over this life
who is coming to us.

DECEMBER 25

Psalm 71:6 Isaiah 7:14 Luke 2:4–7

NATIVITY

The virgin is a mother.
The earth can greet her King.
As stumbling shepherds spread the news,
and shimmering angels withdraw in wonder,
the tiny baby searches for her breast.
Mary smiles, and cradles His reality.
Now Jesus is Emmanuel:
heaven's champion is God-in-flesh.
Christmas has come...

DECEMBER 26 STEPHEN

Psalm 72:14 Isaiah 63:7–10 Acts 7:51–60

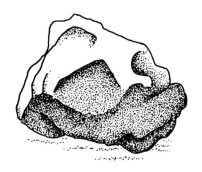

THE STONE

It is an ugly stone, thick and heavy –
but not too heavy to lift, to hurl.
The stone is tinged with red.
We look closely at its shape
but the crowd does not.
The Christian feels its impact.
The stone is one of many.
His face is raised to heaven
as the stone falls
and he sinks to his knees.
The stones smash his body.
Stephen smiles and sleeps.

DECEMBER 27 JOHN THE BELOVED

Psalm 71:18–19 Habakkuk 2:3 John 21:21–25

THE PEN

Mary stored up all these things in her heart
and pondered them. And so did each of us.
And each in our own way told the story.
The story of Jesus can never fully be told.
Each heart He conquers is a new beginning,
and each of us must tell His story;
for His story becomes our own,
even as He has given us His life.

I am the one that Jesus loved.

DECEMBER 28 HOLY INNOCENTS

Psalm 71:4 Exodus 1:15–22 Matthew 2:1–3, 12, 16–18

THE FOETUS

Where is the sound of hope,
the cry of a child that wakes?
The dull, aching, continued breathing
of the mother
becomes a wail of grief,
a weeping for the children
who are no more.
The silent landscape shudders.
God of mercy, light in the darkness,
hold gently to Your heart
the tiny ones we cradle in our prayer,
whose life was over
before it had begun.

DECEMBER 29

Psalm 71:10–12 Exodus 1:22–2:3 Matthew 2:11–15

THE ANGEL

Take the child and His mother down to Egypt's land,
far away from danger, far away from home.
There you may work, there build your Nazareth,
until the time will come when you may return.
Watch well the child who is sleeping now:
the child will be King some day.
Watch well – and we will watch as well.

The child, still sleeping, smiles;
and watching angels wonder, watch and wait.

DECEMBER 30

Psalm 71:17 Hosea 11:1 Matthew 2:19–23

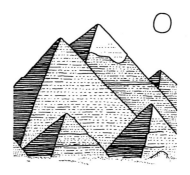

THE PYRAMIDS

Hidden, journeying across the desert.
Hidden, in a strange place.
Hidden, with the gifts and the prophecies buried.
Their time will come, His time of fulfilment.
These are the days of a carpenter's tools,
a trade that can provide for our needs.
There will be more hidden days, hidden years.
His hands will grow to know the feel of wood,
and weigh the impact of the iron nail.
He must be about His father's business.

But how shall we sing the Lord's song
in a strange and weary land?
In waiting and returning
shall we find rest,
and in quietness and confidence
our strength.

DECEMBER 31

Psalm 50:5 1 Samuel 18:1–4; 20:14–17 Luke 22:19–20

THE BREAD AND WINE

The covenant is an exchange (even though it be
rags for royalty and royalty for rags).
It is sealed with blood;
the scars of a blood-brother speak of his faithfulness.
The blood-brother has a right to all his brother possesses,
and even the debts become his.
The enemies of one are the enemies of the other.
The blood-brother speaks his promise:
'This is my body; I will lay down my life on your behalf;
and this my blood I willingly shed for you.'

The covenant is exacted with the sharing of a meal,
the promises repeated in the sharing of bread and wine.
'For all of my days, and for all of my life,
I am no longer my own, but yours,
and you are mine.'

ACKNOWLEDGEMENTS

Text by Andy Raine
© Northumbria Community Trust

Illustrations by Francesca Ross
© Francesca Ross 2013
Used with permission.